THE Reversal PLAN

UNLOCKING THE NEXT LEVEL OF KINGDOM SUCCESS

Patrick Grace
FOREWORD BY BISHOP RONALD L. GODBEE

Studio Griffin
A Publishing Company
www.studiogriffin.net

The Reversal Plan: Unlocking the Next Level of Kingdom Success. Copyright © 2021. Patrick L. Grace

All Rights Reserved. No part of this book may be used or reproduced in any manner whatsoever without written permission except in the case of brief quotations embodied in critical articles and reviews.

For information, contact:
Studio Griffin
A Publishing Company
Garner, North Carolina
studiogriffin@outlook.com
www.studiogriffin.net

Cover Design by Ruth E. Griffin
Images by © adam121/Adobe and © Philip Steury/Adobe

Scripture quotations marked MSG taken from Holy Bible: The Message (the Bible in contemporary language). 2005. Colorado Springs, CO: NavPress.

Scripture quotations marked NIV taken from the Holy Bible, New International Version®. Copyright © 1973, 1978, 1984 International Bible Society. Used by permission of Zondervan. All rights reserved. The "NIV" and "New International Version" trademarks are registered in the United States Patent and Trademark Office by International Bible Society. Use of either trademark requires the permission of International Bible Society.

Scripture quotations marked KJV taken from The Holy Bible, King James Version. New York: American Bible Society: 1999.

Scripture quotations marked NKJV taken from New King James Version Second Edition. Copyright © 1995, 2006 by Thomas Nelson, Inc.

First Edition

ISBN-13: 978-1-954818-00-2

Library of Congress Control Number: 2021903284

1 2 3 4 5 6 7 8 9 10

I dedicate this book to my wife, Latasha Grace. Watching you love and serve with every opportunity given to you has caused me to be a better servant and to serve unselfishly.

And to my son, Richard L. Grace. You are such an incredible young man at the current age of nine. You have a major heart for people, I am excited to watch you grow and serve your generation.

CONTENTS

Foreword	1
Introduction	9
Chapter 1: Matter of The Heart	13
Chapter 2: The Heart Check	19
Chapter 3: Unwrap the Gift	29
Chapter 4: Know the Voice	35
Chapter 5: It's for The People	43
Chapter 6: The Reversal Plan	55
Conclusion	63
Acknowledgements	67
About the Author	69

THE Reversal PLAN

UNLOCKING THE NEXT LEVEL
OF KINGDOM SUCCESS

FOREWORD

My motto has always been, "Serving Into Greatness." If you ever get a communication from me, it will always end with that mantra. Serving is the pathway towards all that we consider to be 'great.' In the Bible, a confident mother comes to Christ and says, "When you come into your kingdom, allow one of my sons to sit on your left and the other one to sit on your right." In Ronald Godbee's translation, Jesus responds, "I'm not in charge of the seating chart of glory, but I have a question: can they drink of the cup that I must drink out of?" The point of the story is that every seat comes with a cup and every crown comes with a cross. Being that 'greatness' comes with the sacrifice of service, we must understand that no one gets the seat without first sipping the cup, no one gets the crown without first carrying the cross, and no one becomes great without the sacrifice of service.

There must be an investment, or a 'seeding of oneself', before there can be an expectation of reward. As we move through the teaching of this powerful book, we will discover the principles that Patrick Grace has placed before us to put us on the path towards greatness. We need tools to build our lives, but not just any tools. My dad used to always tell me, "Son, the right tools are essential to doing a good job. In order to build an incredible house, one must have the right tools." He also taught me that the right tools make the most difficult job easier. With this book, Patrick is giving you the tools to build an incredible life and to provide a rhythmic path toward success.

As you read **The Reversal Plan**, you will discover that one of those tools is a mentor. Mentors matter! Whoever has your ear, holds your future. Show me the person that you call your mentor and I'll show you the pattern and template that you've selected for your life. Your mentors serve as the blueprint for the life that you are trying to build. They plant seeds of wisdom and impart knowledge—that's why they're so important. We need mentors who are mindful not to take our voice, but to help us discover them. Mentors should not take the place of the Lord over us, nor should they exist to celebrate their successes and accomplish-ments to make themselves feel superior to us. They must be willing to be vulnerable and transparent. They should be willing to share the tension that created their trajectory. Mentors can't stand over us but should stand with us to help us discover the brilliance and genius that is lying dormant within. Patrick has the download to help you discover who is deserving of your ear and who should qualify for the privilege of being called your mentor.

One of my mentors always reminds me, "Ronnie, what you touch, you will alter." Remember: those that you give permission to touch your life can alter it for good or for bad. **The Reversal Plan** will give you the tools to take your life back from the hands that have not earned the right to shape your destiny. 'All' success is not good success; someone else's success is not the only tool that you should utilize when identifying your mentor.

Let's use this example: if you're looking for mentorship in the area of marriage, just because someone is a superior basketball player, who has won championships and achieved great fame, but has never been married, doesn't necessarily make them the perfect mentor for you. The garbage man who lives next door but has been married for thirty years may make a far greater mentor than the basketball player with three championship rings, but zero wedding rings. I firmly believe you become what you behold, and if the pathway to success and greatness is service, the ideal mentor has to be someone who exhibits servant leadership and has evidence in their area of expertise. You cannot be mentored by someone who has no mastery in what you're seeking to be mentored in. As you read this book, Patrick will show you how to be selective and purposeful when it comes to discovering who your mentor should be.

The very fact that you picked up **The Reversal Plan** says:

1. You still have time to reverse it!
2. God has a plan for your life that is greater than the one you've known.
3. You have not reached your final level; 'next level' is in your immediate future.
4. God's kingdom plan is better than your carnal plan.

Locked in these pages is the insight you've been waiting for. The answer to prayers that you prayed live just beyond the end of this forward. God has used Patrick Grace to help you unlock and release the God-given brilliance that to-date has remained untapped.

The higher God takes you, the more it becomes incumbent upon you to stay grounded. That grounding will be determined not only by who has your ear in your season of success, but also who had your ear in times of struggle. The servant sips the cup, carries the crown, and becomes the great, but success is sustained by what we read, who we listen to and what wisdom we ingest along the journey. By reading **The Reversal Plan**, consider your success sustained.

Bishop Ronald L. Godbee

Executive Pastor
The River Church

Patrick Grace

The Reversal Plan

Patrick Grace

INTRODUCTION

The one question that everyone has thought on, considered, and even spent money to get the answer to, is simply, "How can I be successful in life?" I believe everyone who is born into the world has the power to determine their success or the lack thereof. Success may vary from person to person, but the fact remains, we all want to live a successful life. Success to one person may be to simply raise their children to be good individuals and have good morals as a family. To someone else, success may be to become the CEO of a Fortune 500 company. Although, we know these are two different ends of the spectrum of life, I believe there are still certain principles and patterns that everyone needs to follow just to reach whatever their respective end of success may be.

I often tell people that the journey to success weighs heavier than the destination of success. How you get there is more important than when or if you arrive. True success is about the lessons that you learn along the way to success. In fact, I would like to suggest that true success is much more than reaching a desired outcome. True success is the growth and knowledge that you gain while trying to reach the goal. The reason I consider that as true success is because those lessons and principles can be passed to another person to obtain their desired outcome of success.

Many times in life, we are so focused on getting to the end that we overlook the lessons that come to teach us and develop us into the person we were created and designed to be. Every day, every situation, and every relationship is filled with lessons that will help us discover more of who we are and what we have locked away inside of us.

In this book, my goal and desire are to enlighten you on a principle that I have learned and have applied in my life. It has opened great doors and taught me important lessons that I am forever grateful for. Everything I do is centered around this one principle. In fact, I will be very trans-parent with you and let you know that my life is built upon this principle. IT IS WHY I LIVE. Every moment of success, every valuable lesson, every remarkable event in my life, I can tie back to this lesson being active in my being and in my ministry. **I wake up every day to activate the principle of SERVING. Yes, that is the key to unlocking the next level of kingdom success.**

What we are about to discover as we take a look into the powerful principle of serving, will cause you to experience success and embrace fulfillment. However, I strongly suggest you understand that this principle is one of the keys that will unlock major doors to success. In Matthew 16:19, Jesus, in His conversation with Peter, said something that is powerful: *"I will give you the keys of the kingdom of heaven." (NIV)* He was not referring to a physical key, but rather a principle or a way of thinking. There are workshops, books, and conferences every day that suggest you will receive the 'keys' to wealth, power, and relationships. Those are not tangible keys that you walk away with at the end of the session, but insight and a different way of thinking. These are keys of thinking that will unlock the next level of living that you desire to reach.

That is my goal and purpose in this book: to enlighten you to think differently as it relates to reaching your goal and desire for success. This is just one of the many keys that you will receive throughout your life journey, but I do believe it's the most important one. So, let's begin our conversation about the power of being a **SERVANT**.

Chapter 1
MATTER OF THE HEART

No one has ever gained success or reached their desired outcome alone. There is always the aid or assistance of someone or others. When living in a society where the number one focus is on self, we have to take time and be honest that the only thing we can successfully do by ourselves is fail. Everything in life that is successful will require the support or aid of someone else (if not a group of people) to be involved.

A teacher cannot be a successful teacher unless there are students to teach. A pastor is not a great pastor away from the involvement of people. A CEO is not successful without the partnerships of those who work in the company and those who patronize the product that is produced. The best surgeon is only the best because of the problems he solves in others. It is the circle of life that we all are in need of each other.

Even if we experience what we feel is negative support, the truth of the matter is that it was still factored into the equation of our process. Take a look at the life of Joseph for a moment. In the book of Genesis chapter 37, we read that Joseph has a dream. Joseph shares it with his brothers but because they already do not have love for him, sharing the dream only makes matters worse between them.

Later, Joseph has another dream and this time he shares the dream with his father and brothers. They do not agree with this dream simply because in it, they are servants to Joseph. Many people look at the position of the servant as they did: one that is downgraded or not of great honor, but I will prove that serving is the key to success.

Though Joseph will one day lead a nation, as a young man, he serves at his father's request. While Joseph's brothers are out working in the field, their father calls for him to go and check on them. The brothers see Joseph coming in their direction, talk among themselves, and get a plan to kill him. However, one brother speaks up and makes a suggestion to not kill Joseph but rather to sell him. Joseph is sold as a slave into Egypt.

Sounds like a messy situation, but there are some great lessons in this story.

In Genesis 39, Joseph is in the house of Potiphar, an officer of Pharaoh, but the hand of the Lord is upon Joseph. He SERVES his master and finds favor and grace in Potiphar's sight, becoming a prosperous man in the process. It is in the midst of the negativity of being betrayed and sold by his brothers that Joseph takes an opportunity to serve and not be selfish. This is a tough position, but you must learn to take what has happened to you and turn it into the blessing of serving others.

We discover that after Joseph becomes the servant to his master, his master puts Joseph in charge of everything that he owns. Being a servant will open doors of promotion that others will not experience, I would like to suggest that it was because of Joseph's heart, but we will deal with that element shortly.

Joseph is in charge over everything that Potiphar has which is a great honor and display of trust that the master has for him.

But in the midst of this, Potiphar's wife sees Joseph and is now lusting after him. She tries her hardest to get Joseph to sleep with her, but because of his loyalty to his master, he runs away, leaving behind his garment.

Please note that a true servant from the heart is always loyal to the one they are serving even in times when they can get benefit and gain for themselves. **Servanthood is a matter of the heart, not a product of actions.** Many will serve others while there is benefit and/or until they can get the gain that they are after. Joseph is so faithful to his servant position that even out of his master's sight, he is still committed to the assignment that was given him. You have to be careful when you have been entrusted with a lot because there will come moments when your desires can cause you to forfeit everything that you have in your hand.

Desires deal with your heart, the part of you that is the real you. I often teach my son that what you desire is a reflection of the condition of your heart. Joseph could have taken advantage of the lustful opportunity with Potiphar's wife. But he understood he would have had to betray the one who entrusted him with his position to serve. There will always be certain things that will remain untouchable by the servant; you have been entrusted with a lot. Know your borders and limitations even with all that you have.

So, Potiphar's wife tells her husband that Joseph tried to sleep with her, and Potiphar has Joseph put into prison. There, in prison, the Lord continues to be with Joseph. Favor is upon him and he is put in charge. Joseph has been from the Pit to Potiphar's house and now in Prison. It is here in prison that Joseph serves the butler and the baker through the interpretations of their own dreams. Have you noticed the common thread that seems to run through Joseph's life in every situation he is put into? He is a **SERVANT** in every one of them.

Joseph's life story gives us a hard truth about being a servant. Many people think that being a servant will always and automatically lead to what initially looks like promotion. But take a closer look into this story and you will discover that serving will also lead you into places that seem worse. Sometimes doing the right thing will put you in a bad place just so you can do the right thing. Promotions rarely come packaged like you desire them to come. More often than not, they come through places, things, and people that you originally would stay away from. Even in what we call a bad or failing place, a true servant will find a way to serve.

Many will argue and suggest that Joseph should have never told his original dream to his family. But I suggest that if he would have not told it, then he would not have experienced all the other serving moments that he had through his journey. The powerful thing about this story is that Joseph's heart is always in the right place, and because of his servant heart, he always gained favor beyond his situation.

Yes! A true servant knows how to be a servant even in their worse situation. Why? Because it is a part of their DNA structure. I want you to study Joseph's life and the success that he gained after the prison to see how he never stopped being a servant. Even to this day, his life is still serving as a testimony to those who are servants.

Chapter 2
THE HEART CHECK

Yes! The first thing we need to examine on our pathway to success is our **Heart**. I am not referring to the one that is pumping blood through your body. The word heart deals with your mind, will, desire, inten-tions, and reason. This is why we have to examine the condition of our heart because everything we do comes from It.

A servant with the right heart will always have a successful outcome, so you have to examine why you do what you do. Many people will serve for a period of time just to receive their desired outcome in life. In other words, they will serve as long as they know the outcome completely benefits them. A true servant heart, though, is not one that is focused on selfish outcomes and gains. This is why it is so important to understand that serving is more than an action, it is a matter of the heart.

Let us unite terminology when talking about servanthood and serving, I do not want to leave it to everyone to input their own concepts which could lead us down several different pathways. **Servant, in my definition, is simply one who possesses the willingness and action to assist someone else without selfish motions or intent.** This is our working definition throughout this book, one that puts us all on the same understanding. With this in mind, we can focus on the conditions of the heart since many people will perform an action without examining their hearts. They will serve but deep down inside, they are operating with selfish motives. I tell people all the time, it is not a matter of what you do, but of why you do it. The 'what' is the by-product and the 'why' is the reason, which is determined by the condition of your heart.

When your 'why' is right, your 'what' will never be taken advantage of, especially when everyone's focus in life is 'not to be taken advantage of.' My spiritual father, Bishop Ronald Godbee, taught me a lesson in 2013 that has forever changed the pattern of my life; he said, *"When your heart is pure, you will always be at the advantage and never be taken advantage of."* Amen.

Our heart has to be focused on the betterment and success of others over our own. The best CEO, Pastor, Teacher, Parent, Supervisor, Friend, or whatever, is the one who is totally focused on serving others and making them better.

> *If you've gotten anything at all out of following Christ, if his love has made any difference in your life, if being in a community of the Spirit means anything to you, if you have a heart, if you care—then do me a favor: Agree with each other, love each other, be deep-spirited friends. Don't push your way to the front; don't sweet-talk your way to the top. Put yourself aside, and help others get ahead. Don't be obsessed with getting your own advantage. Forget yourselves long enough to lend a helping hand. Philippians 2:1-4 (MSG)*

It is expected of us as followers of Christ to always seek the betterment of others and not have the total focus be on just ourselves. I am not saying that we have to totally forget our dreams, goals, and desires, but this scripture teaches us that our focus should be on helping each other rather than thinking of ourselves.

Mahatma Gandhi made a very profound statement: *"The best way to find yourself is to lose yourself in the service of others."* WOW! Such a mind-blowing suggestion that God has so intricately intertwined the fabric of our lives with each other, the only way we can discover who we are is to be sold out in the focus of helping others. It is when I get out of myself that I really find myself. There are a lot of things in my life that I never thought I could do until I was helping others fulfill their desires.

As a pastor, I learn more about who God has empowered me to be by merely helping the people that I serve through daily encounters. Jesus was so focused on bringing pleasure to His heavenly Father that He never desired to fulfill His own will, but it was in fulfilling His Father's desire that Jesus discovered His pleasure. There is a reward that cannot be compared to anything else when we are unselfishly serving our community with the love of Jesus Christ.

Just think about it in your own personal life such as when you are out dining with your family and friends. The more pleasant the server is, the more likely you are to reward them with a gracious tip. On the other side, if the waiter is not pleasant, attentive, and engaging, the less likely you will be to reward them. Every day in life, people seek fulfillment and pleasure, but many fail to realize that what they are searching for is wrapped up in serving.

The more your heart is authentic about serving others, the more people will feel your desire to help them. The reward will always be just what you need for that moment. I recall a friend of mine whom we will call "Heather." Heather was a local waitress in a 'mom and pop' type restaurant. She would leave school and help the owners (we will call them the Brown's) every day, often without pay. This was not because she didn't have anything else to do, but she had a heart to help people, especially the Brown's. It was the summer of 2003. While all other teenagers were making their summer plans, Heather's desire was not to take a break but to work and help the restaurant.

She would get up faithfully, every morning and head to the restaurant to help the owners get the day started. One particular morning, Heather was not feeling well at all, but she pushed her way out of bed to help the older couple. While she had every excuse to stay in bed or just hang out at the local mall, she went to serve instead. So, while serving on this day, a gentleman walked into the restaurant and met the Brown's for lunch. The owners were preparing for their retirement the following year and were meeting with their attorney.

After a great lunch, where they talked about several different business issues, Mr. Brown called for Heather to come to the table and meet the attorney. He asked Heather several questions: How was school? What was she studying? What were her plans for the future? How long had she been helping the Brown's? Heather answered each question, then went back to serving other tables. The attorney and the Brown's finished their meeting and parted ways,

Long story short, the Brown's put it in their plans that Heather would become the new owner of the restaurant when they retired. That is the power of serving with a pure heart and just wanting to see others be successful: the same will always come back to you. It may not come in that form, but it will come in the way and when you need it the most.

For a true servant, there is no job that is too small for you to do. Serving is not about being in the spotlight, having your name known, or getting the reward of a big bank account. Serving produces a reward that nothing in this world can take the place of. It leaves you with a sense of completion, fulfillment, and joy.

I want you to examine your heart and ask yourself the following questions: How is my heart? Is my heart pure enough to serve? Can I serve without recognition? Can I work behind the scenes, even if someone else gets the public fame?

The honest answers to those questions will give you the status of your heart. You have to be honest with yourself before moving forward. The condition of your heart is the energy that flows to everything you do.

Patrick Grace

I have spent all of my life, from my youth until this very moment, serving others and, in every season, there were powerful lessons I learned that developed me into the person I am today.

Becoming a servant is very easy and is something everyone can do. There are a lot of things in life that may hinder or stop us from doing what we desire to do at the moment, but NOTHING can deter you from serving. The step to becoming a servant is simple: just be a problem-solver. Yep, you got it—be a person who seeks to solve problems. I became a problem-solver at the age of ten when I started serving a local church as their musician. Be willing to go the extra step and solve problems because everybody has them.

Servants pay attention to detail, they don't just see the problem, but they look to be the solution to the problem. The local church I served had a problem: they needed a musician, and I had the solution. I was just learning to play the organ, but I was willing to help. I was willing to submit my answer to their problem. I was not looking for any reward but was just willing to help out with what I had. We will deal with this a little later in another chapter, but servants know where to submit their gift.

I could have gone to them with a long list of demands, or with the attitude that they needed me. Had I used that approach to the opportunity, I would have never gained some of the wisdom and experience that I have now. A lot of times, the thing that hinders us in our serving is our attitude or mindset towards serving others. Some feel that to serve someone else is a waste of time or it shows that they are weak. That goes back to the condition of our heart. The greatest person is the one who serves with the right attitude and understands that serving is their greatest asset in life.

You are the strongest when you can put yourself to the side and focus on the development and advancement of others. When you are living a lifestyle of a servant, God will ensure that everything that you need will be taken care of by someone else. When your focus is only on your dreams, visions, goals, and future, you will develop a pattern of walking over others just to get your desires fulfilled. If you notice, anyone who is totally self-centered and self-consumed will experience some level of success, but it will be short-lived and limited. In comparison, someone who lives to serve others every day will be successful on many levels.

Serving is the heartbeat of success; whatever is in the heart will be what flows through your success. When it's full of pride, then pride will be what flows through everything you do. If you have an authentic heart to serve, then authenticity will be the flow of your life. A servant will ensure that their entire team will win and not just them. Their greatest desire is to serve others and watch them grow and exceed in life. Instead of focusing on who is serving you, allow your focus to be on who you serve and how you can be a servant.

Chapter 3
UNWRAP THE GIFT

One of the pessimistic concepts that comes with the idea of serving someone else is the word 'submission.' It tends to lead people down a path that is negative and is often thought of as a weak position. We associate other words with submission such as subjection, authority over, and domination. Therefore, people stray away from the idea of being submitted to anyone that they view as equal or less than who they are. But submission is not a place of weakness. When it is properly viewed and handled, it really is a place of strength and power. To submit means to come up under, support and lift. You find the strength of an individual when they can come up under and lift others above themselves. It is in this place that their inward power is revealed, and the servant heart is operating at peak performance.

Everyone has a gift and purpose that has to be revealed in them, not for their own gain but for the betterment of the world. The worst thing that can happen to a person is to have a gift, talent, and/or a vision at work that has not properly been submitted to someone who can validate their operation. Throughout scripture, we discover that every person who had a great gift at work, at some point in their life, submitted that gift to someone else. In the world today, we call that person a mentor, life coach, pastor, or advisor—someone who can see the gift inside of you and help you open it on a level that you would have never known. Elisha had Elijah, David had Saul, Jesus had John the Baptist, the Disciples had Jesus, and Timothy had Paul, just to name a few.

God has divinely set the person that you need to submit your gift and even your life to. They are waiting for your arrival if they are not already in your life. The purpose of a mentor (which you will see me refer to a lot in this chapter) being in your life is not to be buddies with you but rather to be the person who will push, challenge, and cause you to think outside of your box. The right mentor will not make the process easy for you, but they will make it doable, there is a big difference that you have to understand.

In this chapter, I will let you in on my personal life and my relationship with my mentor who has and still is pushing me beyond my comfort zone for which I am forever grateful. Mentors are all around you and it is possible to have many mentors for different areas of your life. The key to a successful mentor relationship is that you place value on their voice and the wisdom that they share with you. Do not waste a mentor's voice and wisdom—when they share it, show your appreciation through application.

As I have mentioned before, my mentor pushes and challenges me to be better and to go beyond my current borders and boundaries. As I travel and I talk to my peers and different people, there is a common question that I get. I would like to raise an answer to that question now: "How does an individual gain access to their mentor?" My answer is the same every time: "You must understand access is granted." It is not mandatory, but it is conferred by the mentor to the mentee. However, I would like to share a pattern that I have applied and seen at work. It is through this pattern that access is granted.

I strongly believe that every mentee should authentically display a servant's heart, and that through being a servant you will discover the power of paying attention to detail. We have all heard the saying, "the devil is in the details," but I want to argue that statement by saying, "The deliverable is in the details." An excellent waiter, server, or waitress understands the power of detail—they pay ridiculous attention to the one they are serving. This is an attribute that many mentees miss when in contact with their mentor, but it also shows the mentor the position of the mentee's heart. When they fail to pay ridiculous attention to their mentor, it can be determined that they are more focused on their personal gain than valuing the voice of their mentor.

Mentees should always look up to their mentors and, in some cases, desire to model their life in some, if not all, areas. While every mentor is being looked up to, you must understand that every mentor has a need. When the mentee pays ridiculous attention to their mentor, they will discover the need that is there, and they will seek to be the answer to the problem. Every valuable life-changing conversation I have had with my mentor I had it during a moment of serving his needs. I paid attention to the lack that was there in that moment. It could have been something that seemed to be very minor, but that minor moment opened major doors. This taught me to never devalue any opportunity that I am allowed to serve. I gained access to my mentor by merely being a problem-solver and not a problem-starter. If I saw that he needed a bottle of water, I got it, ensuring it was the kind that he liked and how he liked it.

I remember noticing during our mid-week service that my Pastor (my mentor that I am referring to) did not have any one to assist him or what we label as his armor-bearer. I took it upon myself to become the answer to that void. Any time he would have to preach, I would ask his admin to share his calendar and I would arrive at his engage-ments prior to his arrival where I would be ready to serve him, in many (if not most) of the time. He was not aware of me being there awaiting him. No one asked me to do these things, I just enjoyed serving my mentor. As a result, I got the opportunity to see pastoring from behind the scenes and how my mentor handled many different things. You see, the reward of serving is not in the act, but in the position.

It is through observation that you will know how to handle the access you have been given. You never want to gain access and abuse the access that has been granted because of lack of knowledge. I cannot stress enough the importance of giving ridiculous attention. Through simple observation, you will know what your mentor likes and dislikes. The need will always be right in your face if you just pay attention.

Chapter 4
KNOW THE VOICE

The right mentor in the right season will forever change your trajectory, just as the wrong mentor in the wrong season will delay fulfillment. You have to know who is assigned to your life and the season you are in. Will it be comfortable and easy? No. But will it be valuable? Absolutely! When you are confident that you have submitted to the right voice, and you are there to serve at whatever capacity needed. This will cause an unstoppable flow of wisdom to be released. The relationship will yield great harvest in both the mentor and mentee's life since every mentee needs a mentor, and every mentor needs a mentee. The right connection will benefit both beyond their ability to reap a harvest alone.

Mentors are there to help you navigate from where you are to the place you desire to be. The key is to trust their wisdom and value their voice. When my mentor is speaking, I become as a sponge and absorb all that he releases. After paying ridiculous attention and being engaged in the moment that is afforded to you, the next move is to become a ridiculous listener. In some moments, you may hear the same story over and over, to the point you can almost tell it better than they can but listen and engage like it is your first time, every time. It may be in one of those times when the nugget you need the most comes through the story you heard the most.

Listening is the greatest tool you can activate for any relationship. Some of your greatest lessons will come from just listening ridiculously. As an old proverb suggests, "He who has your ear has your life." The Bible teaches us in Romans 10:17 that *faith comes by hearing and hearing by the word of God* (NKJV). This does not apply to just faith elements, but to anything you allow to enter into your hearing. Wisdom comes through listening, but so does fear, and planning for the future. The question you have to ask yourself is, "Who or what do I listen to the most?"

When you listen to the right voice, the one that is assigned to your life, you will begin to unwrap the different layers of who you are.

Think of your life as a gift that is wrapped up—you don't know what is in the box until you begin to remove the layers. That valued voice should position you to discover the real you. They should challenge you in your thinking, strengths, and weaknesses to discover more of yourself. The purpose of a mentor is not to rob you of your identity but to give you the tools to release it. When you become the answer to your mentor's problem, then your mentor becomes the answer to your problem.

My mentor never gave me an answer specifically, but rather positioned me to discover the answer that I was in need of. You and your mentor will do the relation-ship harm when you are always just handed the answer or result. The power of the relationship is when you are positioned to discover for yourself. You are now on the journey to unwrapping the gift that you are, and that gift will be the one that keeps on giving.

As I ponder this lesson, I can't help but think of Elijah in 1 Kings 18. He is at the top of Carmel praying for rain and in prayer Elijah calls for his servant and tells him, "Go up now and look towards the sea." The servant returns to Elijah and reports, "There is nothing." Elijah tells the servant to go back seven times and each time, the report is, "There is nothing." I can imagine around the third time, the servant probably started thinking, "Elijah is losing his mind, got me running back and forth and I keep telling him there is nothing."

Hold up! There is a powerful principle here that I want to deal with. The servant valued the voice of the prophet so much that he remained faithful to the assignment every time the prophet told him to go. There has to be such a value on the voice in your life that you are willing to look foolish, just because you trust that voice.

You have failed as a servant when you begin to insert your feelings into the equation of the relationship. Serving is not about you. You have to learn to serve beyond your feelings and remain faithful to the assignment given. It may be an assignment that you do not like or feel comfortable doing. Elijah's servant went seven times to the same location that the prophet told him to go to. The average person would have looked at the servant and said, "You're crazy for going back and forth." You will have people in your ear telling you opposite of what you are called to do but just remember to value the voice that told you to go.

Elijah never goes to the location but rather sends the servant. Why is that? Could it be that a mentor's job is to stay at the top and communicate to the servant (mentee) where the release will be? Never be afraid to put in the work until you see what your mentor has said will happen. You may not see the release now; your job is to remain in position and serve with a pure heart until you see it.

On the seventh time going out, the servant saw something that he did not see before. His eye had to be trained to see what the mentor said. Remember, your mentor is on a higher level, so you will not see or understand at first everything that is said. It was the consistency of the servant that allowed him to eventually see what the prophet said was coming. The servant went and told Elijah, "I see a cloud the size of a man's hand."

This is so powerful to me; it reveals so many things in those few words. This shows us that great things start with small beginnings. It may not be the big outpour that you want now. It may be small but it's the start of something great.

Next, the story teaches us that our release will come through the hands of man. That is why serving is so important--you don't know which hand is holding your release.

Value the voice of your mentor and you will experience the gift that is in you. As I write this chapter, I can't help but think of another opportunity that I had with my mentor. He held a mentoring class once a week and, of course, I signed up to be included. I just wanted to take hold of every moment I was afforded to be in his presence and to hear wisdom flow from him. I was in class with about twenty-five to thirty other people. Our first assignment was to learn everyone's name in the class, and we had about a full week to learn them. Mind you, we all were attending the same church and had two to three services between each class. The next class came, and he had us go one-by-one and call everyone's name in the class. I patiently waited my turn just knowing that I had this in my pocket. My turn came and to my surprise I did not have it like I thought I did. I missed three names.

At the end of the exercise, my mentor stood back up and said something that shocked me to my core. He said, "Everyone that got it wrong, I know you will be honest and stand up." I stood up along with a few others. Then he said, "You are dismissed from the class, good-bye." My emotions went from 0-1000 in less than three seconds. I was mad, upset, angry, confused and in total disbelief that I just got put out of the mentoring class. Like everyone else, I walked out in my feelings. Before reaching the back door, I heard these words, "Come back." I stopped even though something was telling me to keep walking, go home and save myself the embarrassment. I returned and went back to my seat against that thought.

My mentor continued to talk to the class and said something that stood out to me that night. Even right now as I write this, my soul is being stirred up. He said, "Make sure that is the last time you get put out."

WOW! It was this lesson that hit the button of determination in my life and unwrapped my ability. He could have explained this in class without giving us the experience, but as he later told me, "I had to give you the experience of being put out."

To this day, I hold that experience with high regard. No doubt, the servant felt the same way when Elijah gave him the experience of going back and forth to see what he was trying to show him. If I had not had that experience, I wouldn't have that lesson in my life. Elijah and my mentor both were there to unwrap the gift that was already present. Your mentor is your gift to unwrap and release their blessings to your life.

Chapter 5
IT'S FOR THE PEOPLE

A selfish servant's success will never experience longevity. Everything they do will be centered on them and will give no room for help from others. Anytime there is no room for the involvement from others, your outcome will always be limited to just what you can do. All of us, even in our greatest state, will still have limitations and boundaries that will hinder our forward momentum. I am not saying that we will not have movement and do amazing things, but you will only be able to do what you can do. A real servant's success will outlive them and be passed down for generations to come. Their vision is for more than mere personal gain. Vision that is centered around others is magnetic for support. However, vision that is self-centered is a repellent for help. A servant's perspective is to produce a vision that will bring others to another level of success—again, this is the cycle of life.

Everyone has a vision for success. Before starting your journey, ask yourself: "Is this vision for me or can others benefit from it?" I have learned to take the positions that have been given to me and use them to be a blessing to my community and this world. Yes, I want my wife, family, and church to be blessed by my servanthood, but I also want the world to be blessed by my vision, so it has to live beyond me. You and I may be the ones who have the vision to do and bring forth certain projects, initiatives, and programs, but we will need the help of others to carry it from a vision to visibility. Your support system has to be confident in the fact that you are not here just to produce or be the only one who eats from the labor. Everyone has to see a return on their investment. People do not support or give to a need; they give to and support a vision that will benefit others.

Nehemiah is the perfect example of a vision that is beyond himself. He is the embodiment of a selfless servant. Nehemiah does something that is amazing in his lifetime. So much so that to this day, people still read and use his life for different reasons. He is much more than a book in the Bible. He is someone I recommend for study to anyone who has a servant's heart. I just want to highlight some of his characteristics that will further develop points in this chapter.

Nehemiah was a servant in the king's palace. He had one assignment and that was to be the cupbearer. He was to serve wine to the royal table. The position was of high rank since this person had to be trusted by the king. To be in this position spoke volume to one's character. Trust is the blood that flows through any relationship. The more people trust you, the more they will invest into you, which leads to them giving you more responsibility. The weight of responsibility that you are given is a public display of the level of trust in you.

Though Nehemiah now lived in Susa, his family still resided in Jerusalem, where the walls were broken down and the people were in great distress (Nehemiah 1:3), Nehemiah got word of the condition of his hometown and his family. This became the burden that he carried while in the king's house. Even though he lived in a great place, his heart was broken because his family and community had experienced such calamity.

This is why I call Nehemiah the selfless servant. He could have easily removed himself from the hardship of his people by the mere fact that he was not directly being affected. He could have looked at his life (and who he was connected to) and become numb to the conditions of the people. When your heart is broken by the burden of others, this is a clear indicator that your heart is connected to people. Every great leader makes a lifetime impact when they are genuinely connected to the lives of those they are leading. More often than not, a good leader will carry the people's heavier burden than they carry their own personal burden. In fact, the people's burden becomes their burden. Never allow where you are to remove you from the plight and pain of others.

After getting the news of his hometown, Nehemiah still had to go serve in the capacity that had been given to him. Learn to stay faithful to your assignment without excuses, even when you are carrying a heavy load. Servants do not make excuses as to why they can't serve but they make the adjustment to complete the assignment. While serving the king and queen wine, the king looked at

The Reversal Plan

Nehemiah and realized something was bothering him. This is amazing to me! We talked about paying ridiculous attention as a servant, but here we see it being turned: the king was paying ridiculous attention to the servant. Just when you think no one is watching or paying any attention, God always has the right person looking. This is why we have to learn to remain faithful because faithfulness is the doorway to great things being revealed. When you have every excuse not to be faithful, but instead push beyond it and show up to serve, this is when God has a reward waiting for you.

In Nehemiah 2:2, the king asked Nehemiah, "Why is your countenance sad and are you sick?" Nehemiah took advan-tage of this opportunity and replied to the king, "Why should I be happy when my people are facing the hardest time in their lives?" Never allow your position to take you away from being connected to people. The higher you go in life, the more of a servant you should become. God allowed you to reach a higher place just so that you can be a blessing to those who are not where you are. If you are in the govern-mental sector of life as Nehemiah was your responsibility is not self-gain but for the people. As a pastor, spiritual leader, and in any other position, your focus is not on your own self but that of the people. We are all called to serve PEOPLE. Our life mission and vision should ultimately involve PEOPLE. If it does not involve PEOPLE, it will be buried in the grave with you.

Nehemiah probably got the shock of his life in the reply of the king. "What is your request?" (verse 4) Nehemiah asked if he could get time off to go and see the city. Talk about being a servant at heart! He was not satisfied until he went and experienced what the people were experiencing. The differences between dreams and visions are simply the burden that you have for others beyond you. The burden may be personal, but the blessing has to be for the people. Nehemiah made a sacrifice and took off just to connect with the people in Jerusalem. How far are you willing to go to connect with someone else's pain?

The king approved Nehemiah's time-off request and not just that, he allowed Nehemiah to set the time when he would return back to the king's palace. Therein of itself is a great blessing. When you are faithful to the assignment that is in your hand, you will be able to place demands in those areas of your life that are needed BECAUSE YOU'VE BEEN FAITHFUL.

Nehemiah left but before departing he asked the king for assistance during the trip. The King not only sent a travel letter for Nehemiah to go to Jerusalem but also letters to fund the vision to rebuild the wall. Not only did Nehemiah get to set his return time, now the king was funding the vision that Nehemiah had. When you are faithful to serving someone else's vision, faithful to your assignment and have a vision beyond yourself, God will always ensure that the vision on your heart will be taken care of. You must understand that every moment of serving is just a seed being planted for a great harvest. The harvest is always greater than the seed, but you must first plant the seed through servanthood.

What a reward that Nehemiah received! That is why every moment we get to serve others, we must run and complete it with the right heart. What would have happened if

Nehemiah was so burdened by the plight of his people that he did not show up to serve that day? It is important to under-stand the power of showing up even in your lowest, difficult, and hardest moments. When you decide to show up and serve, even though it is uncomfortable; when you decide to get out of the bed, force a smile and go to work; when you decide, after crying all night, that you are going to help someone else—that is the moment that God begins to allow your reward to head in your direction.

When you are at these difficult moments, if you just push through to serve anyhow, you move from a natural strength to a super-natural power that is beyond you. I often tell people, when you have received your worst doctor's report, that is not the time to go and isolate or insulate yourself with your problems and pain. You immediately go find a way to serve some-one else. My mentor / Bishop taught me, "God does not protect a person, but He protects purpose." As long as the person is found operating in purpose, he will always be protected.

Nehemiah was now given a greater assignment while he was still serving. When you are a true servant, no matter where you go in life, you will find yourself operating as a servant. His success was connected to him being a servant. The more you serve others, the more you secure your success.

A good note to take and remember is that servants are only needed for problems. Whenever you run from problems, you run away from your seed to plant. As a result, you deny your harvest. I like to look at it as this formula: problems are the ground, serving is the seed, and success is the harvest. So, if you want success, the key is to connect with a problem to solve through serving. Then, success is your future.

Let's look back at the life of Nehemiah for a second to get a greater understanding of this principle. We see that when Nehemiah goes to rebuild and bring forth his vision for the wall at Jerusalem, he does not have to do it alone. In fact, he has great support and aid from the people to bring it to pass. They don't just give some of their time, energy, and work but they come with full force, ready to complete the assignment at hand.

Nehemiah 4:6 tells us that *the people had a mind to work* (KJV). This is the harvest from seeds that Nehemiah sowed by just serving in the King's palace. Serving is not a matter of where it's done, but a matter of the attitude and spirit that it is done with. Because of Nehemiah's faithfulness, he reaped the harvest when it came time for the vision that he had. That harvest was FAITHFUL PEOPLE. People who had the mind and spirit to work and build the walls.

When you are faithful in another person's field, then you will reap the harvest of that faithfulness. Personal testimony time: I would serve my leader (and to this day I still serve at whatever capacity is needed) and serve willingly. There is never an assign-ment that is too small or beyond my place to serve. To this day, I can see in the people I serve the same level of commitment, heart, and passion that I have served with. Every moment to serve is really a seed waiting to be planted.

The Reversal Plan

You may say, "Well I don't have the relationship to serve someone such as a king like Nehemiah," or "I'm not that close to my pastor, CEO, local governor or whomever you may view as highly important." The truth of the matter is that serving is not about the position of the individual you are serving. Yes, it is great to serve someone who is what we may perceive has a high rank or position, but the test of a real servant's heart is when you can give your all for the betterment of someone else who may not be able to do it for themselves.

You are consistently afforded an oppor-tunity to be a servant almost every day, it is simply a matter of your perspective. Another understanding of a good servant is the ability to always look for a problem that they can bring a resolution to. Many times, we look for problems to run from instead of looking for problems to run to. Servants are problems-solvers not problem-starters. This is a principle that will work not just in the spiritual sector but in all aspects of life. What do parents, doctors, teachers, employees, pastors, body trainers, mechanics and so many other professions have in common? They all solve problems through serving.

Chapter 6
THE REVERSAL PLAN

Let us now take into consideration a great lesson Jesus taught His disciples that is centered on this same idea and power lesson. In Mark 9:30-37, Jesus is walking with His disciples, who are behind Him having a conversation and arguing among themselves. They are in deep dialogue about which one of them is the greatest. You have to understand that, as Jews, ranking is very important to them. They are really concerned about their status or position in the kingdom.

There are people today who ask the same question. Perhaps we are looking at the different things we have in our life, the position we occupy, the communities we live in, the connections we have. By those things alone, we are quick to assume that we are great, and in some cases, the lack of them will make us feel that we have not achieved a level of greatness. There is this comparison element that often shows up in our journey of life. Comparison is the enemy to your greatness. Whenever you can compare where you are or what you have to someone else, you begin to hinder and stop your progress.

Jesus stops them from comparing and ranking each other to determine what greatness looks like. He then starts to shift their thinking pattern by revealing to them the understanding of how the kingdom of God operates. Here is another powerful lesson to be shared. You may ask why it is a shift in their thinking. The answer to that is simple: prior to Jesus interjecting into their conversation, their understanding was based on what they were accustomed to in the Jewish community.

We discover through the different teach-ings of Jesus that the kingdom of God works in complete opposite to this natural kingdom (world). Jesus tells them in Mark 9:33, *"Anyone who wants to be first must be the very last, and the servant of all* (NIV)." Can you imagine how the disciples were scratching their heads, trying to figure out what Jesus was saying?

"This is completely different from what we know and have been taught," they thought.

The Reversal Plan

"You mean to tell me that the way for us to go up is for us to first go down and serve?"

Yes! This is exactly what Jesus was saying to them—the way up in the kingdom of God is that you first go down. Let's unpack that some more.

One thing I love about Jesus' response to His disciples is how it is not forced but rather how it speaks to one who makes a conscience, deliberate and voluntary choice to deny themselves and put others ahead of them. Not just to deny yourself but to then become servant of ALL. If one is going to be great in the kingdom of God, here is the recipe, that you be last and servant of all. This is not with the under-standing of one being a slave, but one who attends and serves freely to the needs of others. It is not that Jesus is trying to remove us from wanting to better and advance our own personal lives. However, when it comes to the kingdom of God, greatness is only achieved through service not status.

Service and Servant go hand-in-hand. You cannot be a servant without acts of service.

When you discover the ways to serve, you find the service that qualifies you for promotions and elevation. So many times, we are only looking out for ourselves and own personal gains. We fail to provide service that will enhance and better the lives of those we are going through life with. As a Christian, our duty is not just to develop a personal relationship with God, but to live and service our community as we become the hands and feet of Jesus in the earth. Sometimes the only Christ people will see is the Christ in you.

In the world system, the way to advance and get ahead is to be completely focused on you and with a 'by any means necessary' mindset. It is with a 'me-first' and 'me-only' mentality. Here Jesus teaches His dis-ciples, and us, that the kingdom of God works in the reverse. We get ahead through our pushing of others, serving others, denying ourselves, and following His example. Jesus denied Himself to serve those in need, those without, and all people. With that understanding, we can come to the conclusion that if we want the visions, dreams, and passions on our hearts to come to pass, we must find ourselves in the service of helping others. It is the reversal plan of the kingdom.

How many of you are willing to deny yourselves so that someone else can find themselves through you? This is the question I often ask myself. To be honest, there are times I don't feel like doing another act of service, serving that day, or denying myself for someone else. Then I have the thought, "What if this is the seed that I will plant that will produce the harvest I need the most?"

As a pastor, there are times I have to deny myself and travel miles to be with someone during their hardship. I have noticed that every time I personally experienced one of these moments though, there was always a harvest when I needed it most. That is the reversal plan at work. The more I serve when it is beyond my strength, the more strength I get to do more.

Jesus is great not because of the miracles He worked. In fact, the scripture teaches us in John 14:12 that *greater works shall you do* (KJV). He is not great because He was crucified on a cross. There were two others that were crucified right beside Him. Jesus is great because He repeatedly denied Himself to serve humanity into a better place. As a believer and follower of Jesus, every place you go and everything you touch should be better because you came and served humanity.

Jesus is the perfect example of servanthood. He could have forfeited the plan of God many times to gain His own personal status, but He was determined to serve beyond Himself. That is my challenge for you today: now that you have discovered the reversal plan to success, go wrap yourself in service for humanity.

There are many people who are no longer alive, but their names are still ringing in the earth today because they learned to live beyond themselves and serve the greater good. Some of us (if not all of us) are the benefactors of their service to humanity. They went through a lot. Some were even killed in the process, but they remained committed to serving. Now they are great. That is the reversal plan at work.

YOU TOO CAN GO AND BE GREAT. JUST SIMPLY LIVE THE LIFE OF A SERVANT.

Patrick Grace

CONCLUSION

The reversal plan may be to some the road less traveled. In this society, everyone wants things instantly, quickly and to become an overnight success. While the reversal plan may not always grant quick success, it does give you the opportunity to gain sustainable momentum throughout the journey to success. It will give you a fulfillment that cannot be taken away from you, along with lessons that you will teach to generations to come. This path allows you to develop relationships that you will build for a lifetime. Some of my strongest friendships were birthed in moments that I was simply serving. Those things are priceless, and if handled with care, they will continue to increase and propel you higher than you could reach by yourself.

Every morning during my preparation for the day ahead, and even throughout my day, I look for opportunities where I can activate these principles. I wake up every day to serve in some capacity. It could be as simple as opening the door for someone, helping someone with a problem, or allowing someone in the store to go ahead of me in the checkout line. You may not look at these things as opportunities to serve but indeed they are because you're putting someone else ahead of you. Never belittle any opportunity to help or serve someone else. Remember, we all have a need.

The kingdom of God works in the reverse and that is how we gain promotions, increase, and make a lasting effect on this world. Each year, I ask my leadership team: "Who will be the biggest servant this year?" Not who wants a promotion, not who wants notoriety but who wants to serve and who will find ways to be a servant.

If you don't have anything else, you will always have an opportunity to be a servant. Remember what Jesus said in Matthew 25:35-36: *"For I was hungry, and you gave me something to eat, I was thirsty, and you gave me something to drink, I was a stranger and you invited me in, I needed clothes and you clothed me, I was sick, and you looked after me, I was in prison and you came to visit me'"* (NIV). What Jesus was teaching us through these statements is that there is always a need and you can become the servant to the need. Serving is your security because as long as you are serving a need, you will never become that need.

Put yourself in the mind frame every day that you are here not to be served but to serve. When you serve with the right heart, when you allow your service to benefit the people, and when you are surrounded by the right voice, there will be a peace and fulfillment released into your life that will propel and catapult you to a place that you would have never imagined without serving.

In closing, think of it like this: the highest building can only be supported by how deep it is in the ground. They have to build in reverse—they have to go down before they can go high. Let your life be that of a construction site: enjoy working in the reverse. Serve your way to the highest peak of life.

Patrick Grace

ACKNOWLEDGEMENTS

With a grateful heart, I would like to thank everyone who allowed me to bounce different concepts and ideas off of them, and those who would not let me stop until I finished this work. Thank you so much for being great in this journey. People are now understanding another key to success in the kingdom because of your involvement in this process. From the bottom of my heart, thank you.

Patrick Grace

ABOUT THE AUTHOR

Patrick L. Grace is a native of Raeford, North Carolina but now resides in Raleigh, North Carolina with his lovely wife, Mrs. Latasha Grace. They are the parents of Richard L. Grace. Patrick has a heart for loving the people of God and wanting to see them grow stronger and deeper in God and fulfill their God-given purpose. He has operated in ministry since childhood and has served as minister of music at a few local churches as well as choir director for some of the local community choirs.

Patrick's expository teaching, charismatic preaching and powerful anointing has caused him to travel extensively, sharing, and depositing wisdom into the lives and hearts of God's people. He has been afforded great ministry opportunities and preaching on many platforms, conducted several workshops for The Union Baptist Association in Fayetteville, North Carolina, and he has served on several boards of directors. He has been a guest on several discussion panels dealing with different subjects as it relates to the Body of Christ and Young Adults. He was one of the co-hosts of a worldwide radio talk show entitled, 'What's the Fresh Word?'

In 2016, under the leadership of Bishop Ronald L. Godbee at The River Church in Durham, North Carolina, Patrick and Latasha were ordained as Pastors. At this point in ministry, Bishop Godbee, through the spirit of God, released them both from The River Church to establish what would be known as The Advance Church back in Patrick's hometown. In January 2017, The Advance Church was brought forth in the earth, a place and people that became Real, Relevant, and Relational.

After being faithful to the assignment and ministry, God commissioned them to go to the next level. Solely out of obedience and submission to the will of God, Patrick took the members of The Advance Church and connected them to the vision that was established by Dr. Robert L. and Lady Gladys Bronson at St. Paul Full Gospel Baptist Church in Fayetteville, North Carolina.

Today, Pastor Patrick and Lady Tasha, also known as 'Pastor P & Lady T,' faithfully serve the people of God and lead them as their Pastors to a higher level in God. The heart of the ministry is to serve each other and build up the community through the power of God. St. Paul is experiencing steady and healthy growth under their leadership and is moving towards being a model ministry.

Patrick Grace

www.ingramcontent.com/pod-product-compliance
Lightning Source LLC
Chambersburg PA
CBHW071509070526
44578CB00001B/484